D0096337

This Book Belongs To

____

Trendy Printing

Library

Made in the USA
Monee, IL
16 June 2022

98161223R00056